THE PASSION OF OUR LORD JESUS CHRIST

THE PASSION OF OUR LORD JESUS CHRIST

ACCORDING TO THE FOUR EVANGELISTS

With an introduction from St Francis De Sales

CANA PRESS

All Scripture taken from the Douay Rheims Challoner translation.

Excerpt of St Francis De Sales taken from the translation of Dom Mackey, published by Burns & Oates Ltd., 1884.

Cana Press © 2024

All rights reserved.
No part of this book may be reproduced or transmitted, in any form or by any means, without permission.

For information, address:
PO Box 85,
Colebrook,
Tasmania, 7027,
Australia

notredamemonastery.org

ISBN

978-0-6454653-8-9

CONTENTS

Meditating on the Passion
  St Francis De Sales 1
The Passion of Our Lord Jesus Christ
  according to St Matthew 5
The Passion of Our Lord Jesus Christ
  according to St Mark 21
The Passion of Our Lord Jesus Christ
  according to St Luke 35
The Passion of Our Lord Jesus Christ
  according to St John 49

MEDITATING ON THE PASSION

ST FRANCIS DE SALES

The death and passion of Our Lord is the sweetest and most constraining motive that can animate our hearts in this mortal life: and it is the very truth, that mystical bees make their most excellent honey within the wounds of this Lion of the tribe of Judah, slain, rent and torn upon the Mount of Calvary. And the children of the cross glory in their admirable problem, which the world understands not: Out of death, the eater of all, has come forth the meat of our consolation; and out of death, strong above all, has come forth the sweetness of the honey of our love. (Judges 14:14) O Jesus, my Saviour, how love-worthy is thy death, since it is the sovereign effect of thy love!

So, in the glory of heaven above, next to the Divine goodness known and considered in itself, Our Saviour's death shall most powerfully ravish the blessed spirits in the loving of God. As a sign whereof, in the Transfiguration, where we have a glimpse of heaven, Moses and Elias *talked with Our Saviour of the Excess* (*Excessum*, Luke 9:31) which he was to accomplish in Jerusalem. But of what excess, if not of that excess of love by which life was forced from the lover, to be bestowed on the well-beloved? So that in the eternal canticle I imagine to myself that this joyous exclamation will be repeated every moment:

> Live, Jesus live, whose death doth prove,
> The might supreme of heavenly love.

Mount Calvary is the mount of lovers. All love that takes not its beginning from Our Saviour's Passion is frivolous and dangerous. Unhappy is death without the love of the Saviour, unhappy is love without the death of the Saviour! Love and death are so mingled in the Passion of Our Saviour that we cannot have the one in our heart without the other. Upon Calvary one cannot have life without love, nor love without the death of Our Redeemer. But, except there, all is either eternal death or eternal love: and all Christian wisdom consists in choosing rightly.

During this mortal life we must choose eternal love or eternal death, there is no middle choice.

O eternal love, my soul desires and makes choice of thee eternally! Ah! come, Holy Spirit and inflame our hearts with thy love! To love or to die! To die and to love! To die to all other love in order to live to Jesus's love, that we may not die eternally, but that, living in thy eternal love, O Saviour of our souls we may eternally sing: *Vive Jésus!* I love Jesus. Live Jesus whom I love! I love Jesus, who lives and reigns for ever and ever. Amen.

Excerpt from St Francis De Sales, *The Treatise on the Love of God*, Book XII, Chapter 13, Translated by Dom Mackey, O.S.B., 1884.

THE PASSION OF OUR LORD JESUS CHRIST ACCORDING TO ST MATTHEW

CHAPTER 26

And it came to pass, when Jesus had ended all these words, he said to his disciples: ²You know that after two days shall be the pasch: and the Son of man shall be delivered up to be crucified.

³Then were gathered together the chief priests and ancients of the people, into the court of the high priest, who was called Caiphas: ⁴And they consulted together that by subtilty they might apprehend Jesus and put him to death. ⁵But they said: Not on the festival day, lest perhaps there should be a tumult among the people.

⁶And when Jesus was in Bethania, in the house of Simon the leper, ⁷There came to him

a woman having an alabaster box of precious ointment and poured it on his head as he was at table. ⁸And the disciples seeing it had indignation, saying: To what purpose is this waste? ⁹For this might have been sold for much and given to the poor.

¹⁰And Jesus knowing it, said to them: Why do you trouble this woman? For she hath wrought a good work upon me. ¹¹For the poor you have always with you: but me you have not always.* ¹²For she in pouring this ointment on my body hath done it for my burial. ¹³Amen I say to you, wheresoever this gospel shall be preached in the whole world, that also which she hath done shall be told for a memory of her.

¹⁴Then went one of the twelve, who was called Judas Iscariot, to the chief priests. ¹⁵And said to them: What will you give me, and I will deliver him unto you? But they appointed him thirty pieces of silver. ¹⁶And from thenceforth he sought opportunity to betray him.

* *Me you have not always...* Viz., in a visible manner, as when conversant here on earth; and as we have the poor, whom we may daily assist and relieve.

¹⁷And on the first day of the Azymes,* the disciples came to Jesus, saying: Where wilt thou that we prepare for thee to eat the pasch?† ¹⁸But Jesus said: Go ye into the city to a certain man and say to him: The master saith, My time is near at hand. With thee I make the pasch with my disciples. ¹⁹And the disciples did as Jesus appointed to them: and they prepared the pasch.

²⁰But when it was evening, he sat down with his twelve disciples. ²¹And whilst they were eating, he said: Amen I say to you that one of you is about to betray me. ²²And they being very much troubled began every one to say: Is it I, Lord? ²³But he answering said: He that dippeth his hand with me in the dish, he shall betray me. ²⁴The Son of man indeed goeth, as it is written of him. But woe to that man by whom the Son of man shall be betrayed. It were better for him, if that man had not been born. ²⁵And Judas that betrayed him answering, said: Is it I, Rabbi? He saith to him: Thou hast said it.

²⁶And whilst they were at supper, Jesus took bread and blessed and broke and gave to his

* *Azymes...* Feast of the unleavened bread.
† *Pasch...* The paschal lamb.

disciples and said: Take ye and eat. This is my body.* ²⁷And taking the chalice, he gave thanks and gave to them, saying: Drink ye all of this.† ²⁸For this is my blood of the new testament,‡ which shall be shed for many unto remission of sins. ²⁹And I say to you, I will not drink from

* *This is my body...* He does not say, This is the figure of my body—but This is my body. (2 Council of Nice, Act:6.) Neither does he say in this, or with this is my body; but absolutely, This is my body: which plainly implies transubstantiation.

† *Drink ye all of this...* This was spoken to the twelve apostles; who were the all then present; and they all drank of it, says St. Mark 14:23. But it no ways follows from these words spoken to the apostles, that all the faithful are here commanded to drink of the chalice; any more than that all the faithful are commanded to consecrate, offer and administer this sacrament; because Christ upon this same occasion, and at the same time, bid the apostles do so; in these words, St. Luke 22:19, Do this for a commemoration of me.

‡ *Blood of the new testament...* As the old testament was dedicated with the blood of victims, by Moses, in these words: This is the blood of the testament, etc., Heb. 9:20; so here is the dedication and institution of the new testament, in the blood of Christ, here mystically shed by these words: This is the blood of the new testament, etc.

henceforth of this fruit of the vine* until that day when I shall drink it with you new in the kingdom of my Father.

³⁰And a hymn being said, they went out unto mount Olivet. ³¹Then Jesus saith to them: All you shall be scandalized in me this night. For it is written: I will strike the shepherd: and the sheep of the flock shall be dispersed.† ³²But after I shall be risen again, I will go before you into Galilee. ³³And Peter answering, said to him: Although all shall be scandalized in thee, I will never be scandalized. ³⁴Jesus said to him: Amen I say to thee that in this night before the cock crow, thou wilt deny me thrice. ³⁵Peter saith to him: Yea, though I should die with thee, I will not deny thee. And in like manner said all the disciples.

* *Fruit of the vine...* These words, by the account of St. Luke 22:18, were not spoken of the sacramental cup, but of the wine that was drunk with the paschal lamb. Though the sacramental cup might also be called the fruit of the vine, because it was consecrated from wine, and retains the likeness, and all the accidents or qualities of wine.

†*Scandalized in me, etc...* Forasmuch as my being apprehended shall make you all run away and forsake me.

[36]Then Jesus came with them into a country place which is called Gethsemani. And he said to his disciples: Sit you here, till I go yonder and pray. [37]And taking with him Peter and the two sons of Zebedee, he began to grow sorrowful and to be sad. [38]Then he saith to them: My soul is sorrowful even unto death. Stay you here and watch with me. [39]And going a little further, he fell upon his face, praying and saying: My Father, if it be possible, let this chalice pass from me. Nevertheless, not as I will but as thou wilt.

[40]And he cometh to his disciples and findeth them asleep. And he saith to Peter: What? Could you not watch one hour with me? [41]Watch ye: and pray that ye enter not into temptation. The spirit indeed is willing, but the flesh weak. [42]Again the second time, he went and prayed, saying: My Father, if this chalice may not pass away, but I must drink it, thy will be done. [43]And he cometh again and findeth them sleeping: for their eyes were heavy. [44]And leaving them, he went again: and he prayed the third time, saying the selfsame word. [45]Then he cometh to his disciples and said to them: Sleep ye now and take your rest. Behold the hour is at hand: and

the Son of man shall be betrayed into the hands of sinners. ⁴⁶Rise: let us go. Behold he is at hand that will betray me. ⁴⁷As he yet spoke, behold Judas, one of the twelve, came, and with him a great multitude with swords and clubs, sent from the chief priests and the ancients of the people. ⁴⁸And he that betrayed him gave them a sign, saying: Whomsoever I shall kiss, that is he. Hold him fast. ⁴⁹And forthwith coming to Jesus, he said: Hail, Rabbi. And he kissed him. ⁵⁰And Jesus said to him: Friend, whereto art thou come? Then they came up and laid hands on Jesus and held him.

⁵¹And behold one of them that were with Jesus, stretching forth his hand, drew out his sword: and striking the servant of the high priest, cut off his ear. ⁵²Then Jesus saith to him: Put up again thy sword into its place: for all that take the sword shall perish with the sword. ⁵³Thinkest thou that I cannot ask my Father, and he will give me presently more than twelve legions of angels? ⁵⁴How then shall the scriptures be fulfilled, that so it must be done?

⁵⁵In that same hour, Jesus said to the multitudes: You are come out, as it were to a robber,

with swords and clubs to apprehend me. I sat daily with you, teaching in the temple: and you laid not hands on me. ⁵⁶Now all this was done that the scriptures of the prophets might be fulfilled. Then the disciples, all leaving him, fled.

⁵⁷But they holding Jesus led him to Caiphas the high priest, where the scribes and the ancients were assembled. ⁵⁸And Peter followed him afar off, even to the court of the high priest, And going in, he sat with the servants, that he might see the end. ⁵⁹And the chief priests and the whole council sought false witness against Jesus, that they might put him to death. ⁶⁰And they found not, whereas many false witnesses had come in. And last of all there came two false witnesses: ⁶¹And they said: This man said, I am able to destroy the temple of God and after three days to rebuild it.

⁶²And the high priest rising up, said to him: Answerest thou nothing to the things which these witness against thee? ⁶³But Jesus held his peace. And the high priest said to him: I adjure thee by the living God, that thou tell us if thou be the Christ the Son of God. ⁶⁴Jesus saith to him: Thou hast said it. Nevertheless I say to

you, hereafter you shall see the Son of man sitting on the right hand of the power of God and coming in the clouds of heaven.

⁶⁵Then the high priest rent his garments, saying: He hath blasphemed: What further need have we of witnesses? Behold, now you have heard the blasphemy. ⁶⁶What think you? But they answering, said: He is guilty of death. ⁶⁷Then did they spit in his face and buffeted him. And others struck his face with the palms of their hands, ⁶⁸Saying: Prophesy unto us, O Christ. Who is he that struck thee?

⁶⁹But Peter sat without in the court. And there came to him a servant maid, saying: Thou also wast with Jesus the Galilean. ⁷⁰But he denied before them all, saying: I know not what thou sayest. ⁷¹And as he went out of the gate, another maid saw him; and she saith to them that were there: This man also was with Jesus of Nazareth. ⁷²And again he denied with an oath: I know not the man. ⁷³And after a little while, they came that stood by and said to Peter: Surely thou also art one of them. For even thy speech doth discover thee. ⁷⁴Then he began to curse and to swear that he knew not the man.

And immediately the cock crew. ⁷⁵And Peter remembered the word of Jesus which he had said: Before the cock crow, thou wilt deny me thrice. And going forth, he wept bitterly.

CHAPTER 27

And when morning was come, all the chief priests and ancients of the people took counsel against Jesus, that they might put him to death. ²And they brought him bound and delivered him to Pontius Pilate the governor.

³Then Judas, who betrayed him, seeing that he was condemned, repenting himself, brought back the thirty pieces of silver to the chief priests and ancients, ⁴Saying: I have sinned in betraying innocent blood. But they said: What is that to us? Look thou to it. ⁵And casting down the pieces of silver in the temple, he departed and went and hanged himself with an halter.

⁶But the chief priests having taken the pieces of silver, said: It is not lawful to put them into the corbona,* because it is the price of blood. ⁷And after they had consulted together,

* *Corbona...* A place in the temple where the people put in their gifts or offerings.

they bought with them the potter's field, to be a burying place for strangers. ⁸For this cause that field was called Haceldama, that is, the field of blood, even to this day. ⁹Then was fulfilled that which was spoken by Jeremias the prophet, saying: And they took the thirty pieces of silver, the price of him that was prized, whom they prized of the children of Israel. ¹⁰And they gave them unto the potter's field, as the Lord appointed to me.

¹¹And Jesus stood before the governor, and the governor asked him, saying: Art thou the king of the Jews? Jesus saith to him: Thou sayest it. ¹²And when he was accused by the chief priests and ancients, he answered nothing. ¹³Then Pilate saith to him: Dost not thou hear how great testimonies they allege against thee? ¹⁴And he answered him to never a word, so that the governor wondered exceedingly.

¹⁵Now upon the solemn day the governor was accustomed to release to the people one prisoner, whom they would. ¹⁶And he had then a notorious prisoner that was called Barabbas. ¹⁷They therefore being gathered together, Pilate said: Whom will you that I release to You:

Barabbas, or Jesus that is called Christ? [18]For he knew that for envy they had delivered him. [19]And as he was sitting in the place of judgment, his wife sent to him, saying: Have thou nothing to do with that just man; for I have suffered many things this day in a dream because of him. [20]But the chief priests and ancients persuaded the people that they should ask Barabbas and make Jesus away. [21]And the governor answering, said to them: Whether will you of the two to be released unto you? But they said: Barabbas. [22]Pilate saith to them: What shall I do then with Jesus that is called Christ? They say all: Let him be crucified. [23]The governor said to them: Why, what evil hath he done? But they cried out the more, saying: Let him be crucified.

[24]And Pilate seeing that he prevailed nothing, but that rather a tumult was made, taking water washed his hands before the people, saying: I am innocent of the blood of this just man. Look you to it. [25]And the whole people answering, said: His blood be upon us and upon our children.

[26]Then he released to them Barabbas: and having scourged Jesus, delivered him unto them to be crucified. [27]Then the soldiers of the gover-

nor, taking Jesus into the hall, gathered together unto him the whole band. ²⁸And stripping him, they put a scarlet cloak about him. ²⁹And platting a crown of thorns, they put it upon his head, and a reed in his right hand. And bowing the knee before him, they mocked him, saying: Hail, King of the Jews. ³⁰And spitting upon him, they took the reed and struck his head.

³¹And after they had mocked him, they took off the cloak from him and put on him his own garments and led him away to crucify him. ³²And going out, they found a man of Cyrene, named Simon: him they forced to take up his cross. ³³And they came to the place that is called Golgotha, which is the place of Calvary.

³⁴And they gave him wine to drink mingled with gall. And when he had tasted, he would not drink. ³⁵And after they had crucified him, they divided his garments, casting lots; that it might be fulfilled which was spoken by the prophet, saying: They divided my garments among them; and upon my vesture they cast lots. ³⁶And they sat and watched him. ³⁷And they put over his head his cause written: THIS IS JESUS THE KING OF THE JEWS.

³⁸Then were crucified with him two thieves: one on the right hand and one on the left. ³⁹And they that passed by blasphemed him, wagging their heads, ⁴⁰And saying: Vah, thou that destroyest the temple of God and in three days dost rebuild it: save thy own self. If thou be the Son of God, come down from the cross. ⁴¹In like manner also the chief priests, with the scribes and ancients, mocking said: ⁴²He saved others: himself he cannot save. If he be the king of Israel, let him now come down from the cross: and we will believe him. ⁴³He trusted in God: let him now deliver him if he will have him. For he said: I am the Son of God. ⁴⁴And the selfsame thing the thieves also that were crucified with him reproached him with.

⁴⁵Now from the sixth hour, there was darkness over the whole earth, until the ninth hour. ⁴⁶And about the ninth hour, Jesus cried with a loud voice, saying: Eli, Eli, lamma sabacthani? That is, My God, My God, why hast thou forsaken me? ⁴⁷And some that stood there and heard said: This man calleth Elias. ⁴⁸And immediately one of them running took a sponge and filled it with vinegar and put it on a reed

and gave him to drink. ^{49}And the others said: Let be. Let us see whether Elias will come to deliver him. ^{50}And Jesus again crying with a loud voice, yielded up the ghost.

^{51}And behold the veil of the temple was rent in two from the top even to the bottom: and the earth quaked and the rocks were rent. ^{52}And the graves were opened: and many bodies of the saints that had slept arose, ^{53}And coming out of the tombs after his resurrection, came into the holy city and appeared to many. ^{54}Now the centurion and they that were with him watching Jesus, having seen the earthquake and the things that were done, were sore afraid, saying: Indeed this was the Son of God. ^{55}And there were there many women afar off, who had followed Jesus from Galilee, ministering unto him: ^{56}Among whom was Mary Magdalen and Mary the mother of James and Joseph and the mother of the sons of Zebedee.

^{57}And when it was evening, there came a certain rich man of Arimathea, named Joseph, who also himself was a disciple of Jesus. ^{58}He went to Pilate and asked the body of Jesus. Then Pilate commanded that the body should be delivered.

⁵⁹And Joseph taking the body wrapped it up in a clean linen cloth: ⁶⁰And laid it in his own new monument, which he had hewed out in a rock. And he rolled a great stone to the door of the monument and went his way. ⁶¹And there was there Mary Magdalen and the other Mary, sitting over against the sepulchre.

⁶²And the next day, which followed the day of preparation,* the chief priests and the Pharisees came together to Pilate, ⁶³Saying: Sir, we have remembered, that that seducer said, while he was yet alive: After three days I will rise again. ⁶⁴Command therefore the sepulchre to be guarded until the third day: lest perhaps his disciples come and steal him away and say to the people: He is risen from the dead. And the last error shall be worse than the first. ⁶⁵Pilate saith to them: You have a guard. Go, guard it as you know. ⁶⁶And they departing, made the sepulchre sure, sealing the stone and setting guards.

---

* *The day of preparation...* The eve of the sabbath; so called, because on that day they prepared all things necessary; not being allowed so much as to dress their meat on the sabbath day.

THE PASSION OF OUR LORD JESUS CHRIST ACCORDING TO ST MARK

CHAPTER 14

Now the feast of the pasch and of the Azymes* was after two days: and the chief priests and the scribes sought how they might by some wile lay hold on him and kill him. ²But they said: Not on the festival day, lest there should be a tumult among the people.

³And when he was in Bethania, in the house of Simon the leper, and was at meat, there came a woman having an alabaster box of ointment of precious spikenard. And breaking the alabaster box, she poured it out upon his head. ⁴Now there were some that had indignation within

* *Azymes...* That is, the feast of the unleavened bread.

themselves and said: Why was this waste of the ointment made? ⁵For this ointment might have been sold for more than three hundred pence and given to the poor. And they murmured against her.

⁶But Jesus said: Let her alone. Why do you molest her? She hath wrought a good work upon me. ⁷For the poor you have always with you: and whensoever you will, you may do them good: but me you have not always. ⁸She hath done what she could: she is come beforehand to anoint my body for the burial. ⁹Amen, I say to you, wheresoever this gospel shall be preached in the whole world, that also which she hath done shall be told for a memorial of her.

¹⁰And Judas Iscariot, one of the twelve, went to the chief priests, to betray him to them. ¹¹Who hearing it were glad: and they promised him they would give him money. And he sought how he might conveniently betray him.

¹²Now on the first day of the unleavened bread, when they sacrificed the pasch, the disciples say to him: Whither wilt thou that we go and prepare for thee to eat the pasch? ¹³And he sendeth two of his disciples and saith to them: Go ye into the

city; and there shall meet you a man carrying a pitcher of water. Follow him. ¹⁴And whithersoever he shall go in, say to the master of the house, The master saith, Where is my refectory, where I may eat the pasch with my disciples? ¹⁵And he will shew you a large dining room furnished. And there prepare ye for us. ¹⁶And his disciples went their way and came into the city. And they found as he had told them: and they prepared the pasch.

¹⁷And when evening was come, he cometh with the twelve. ¹⁸And when they were at table and eating, Jesus saith: Amen I say to you, one of you that eateth with me shall betray me. ¹⁹But they began to be sorrowful and to say to him, one by one: Is it I? ²⁰Who saith to them: One of the twelve, who dippeth with me his hand in the dish. ²¹And the Son of man indeed goeth, as it is written of him: but woe to that man by whom the Son of man shall be betrayed. It were better for him, if that man had not been born.

²²And whilst they were eating, Jesus took bread; and blessing, broke and gave to them and said: Take ye. This is my body. ²³And having taken the chalice, giving thanks, he gave it to them. And they all drank of it. ²⁴And he said

to them: This is my blood of the new testament, which shall be shed for many. ²⁵Amen I say to you that I will drink no more of the fruit of the vine until that day when I shall drink it new in the kingdom of God.

²⁶And when they had sung an hymn, they went forth to the mount of Olives. ²⁷And Jesus saith to them: You will all be scandalized in my regard this night. For it is written: I will strike the shepherd, and the sheep shall be dispersed. ²⁸But after I shall be risen again, I will go before you into Galilee. ²⁹But Peter saith to him: Although all shall be scandalized in thee, yet not I. ³⁰And Jesus saith to him: Amen I say to thee, to-day, even in this night, before the cock crow twice, thou shalt deny me thrice.* ³¹But he spoke the more vehemently: Although I should die together with thee, I will not deny thee. And in like manner also said they all.

* *Crow twice...* The cocks crow at two different times of the night; viz., about midnight for the first time; and then about the time commonly called the cock crowing; and this was the cock crowing our Saviour spoke of; and therefore the other Evangelists take no notice of the first crowing.

³²And they came to a farm called Gethsemani. And he saith to his disciples: Sit you here, while I pray. ³³And he taketh Peter and James and John with him: and he began to fear and to be heavy. ³⁴And he saith to them: My soul is sorrowful even unto death. Stay you here and watch. ³⁵And when he was gone forward a little, he fell flat on the ground: and he prayed that, if it might be, the hour might pass from him. ³⁶And he saith: Abba, Father, all things are possible to thee: remove this chalice from me; but not what I will, but what thou wilt.

³⁷And he cometh and findeth them sleeping. And he saith to Peter: Simon, sleepest thou? Couldst thou not watch one hour? ³⁸Watch ye: and pray that you enter not into temptation. The spirit indeed is willing, but the flesh is weak. ³⁹And going away again, he prayed, saying the same words.

⁴⁰And when he returned, he found them again asleep (for their eyes were heavy): and they knew not what to answer him. ⁴¹And he cometh the third time and saith to them: Sleep ye now and take your rest. It is enough. The hour is come: behold the Son of man shall be

betrayed into the hands of sinners. ⁴²Rise up: let us go. Behold, he that will betray me is at hand.

⁴³And while he was yet speaking, cometh Judas Iscariot, one of the twelve: and with him a great multitude with swords and staves, from the chief priests and the scribes and the ancients. ⁴⁴And he that betrayed him had given them a sign, saying: Whomsoever I shall kiss, that is he. Lay hold on him: and lead him away carefully. ⁴⁵And when he was come, immediately going up to him he saith: Hail, Rabbi! And he kissed him. ⁴⁶But they laid hands on him and held him.

⁴⁷And one of them that stood by, drawing a sword, struck a servant of the chief priest and cut off his ear. ⁴⁸And Jesus answering, said to them: Are you come out as to a robber, with swords and staves to apprehend me? ⁴⁹I was daily with you in the temple teaching: and you did not lay hands on me. But that the scriptures may be fulfilled.

⁵⁰Then his disciples, leaving him, all fled away. ⁵¹And a certain young man followed him, having a linen cloth cast about his naked body. And they laid hold on him. ⁵²But he, casting off the linen cloth, fled from them naked.

⁵³And they brought Jesus to the high priest. And all the priests and the scribes and the ancients assembled together. ⁵⁴And Peter followed him afar off, even into the court of the high priest. And he sat with the servants at the fire and warmed himself. ⁵⁵And the chief priests and all the council sought for evidence against Jesus, that they might put him to death: and found none. ⁵⁶For many bore false witness against him: and their evidences were not agreeing. ⁵⁷And some rising up, bore false witness against him, saying: ⁵⁸We heard him say, I will destroy this temple made with hands and within three days I will build another not made with hands. ⁵⁹And their witness did not agree.

⁶⁰And the high priest rising up in the midst, asked Jesus, saying: Answerest thou nothing to the things that are laid to thy charge by these men? ⁶¹But he held his peace and answered nothing. Again the high priest asked him and said to him: Art thou the Christ, the Son of the Blessed God? ⁶²And Jesus said to him: I am. And you shall see the Son of man sitting on the right hand of the power of God and coming with the clouds of heaven.

⁶³Then the high priest rending his garments, saith: What need we any further witnesses? ⁶⁴You have heard the blasphemy. What think you? Who all condemned him to be guilty of death. ⁶⁵And some began to spit on him and to cover his face and to buffet him and to say unto him: Prophesy. And the servants struck him with the palms of their hands.

⁶⁶Now when Peter was in the court below, there cometh one of the maidservants of the high priest. ⁶⁷And when she had seen Peter warming himself looking on him, she saith: Thou also wast with Jesus of Nazareth. ⁶⁸But he denied, saying: I neither know nor understand what thou sayest. And he went forth before the court; and the cock crew. ⁶⁹And again a maidservant seeing him, began to say to the standers by: This is one of them. ⁷⁰But he denied again. And after a, while they that stood by said again to Peter: Surely thou art one of them; for thou art also a Galilean. ⁷¹But he began o curse and to swear, saying: I know not this man of whom you speak. ⁷²And immediately the cock crew again. And Peter remembered the word that Jesus had

said unto him: Before the cock crow twice, thou shalt thrice deny me. And he began to weep,

CHAPTER 15

And straightway in the morning, the chief priests holding a consultation with the ancients and the scribes and the whole council, binding Jesus, led him away and delivered him to Pilate. ²And Pilate asked him: Art thou the king of the Jews? But he answering, saith to him: Thou sayest it. ³And the chief priests accused him in many things. ⁴And Pilate again asked him, saying: Answerest thou nothing? Behold in how many things they accuse thee. ⁵But Jesus still answered nothing: so that Pilate wondered.

⁶Now on the festival day he was wont to release unto them one of the prisoners, whomsoever they demanded. ⁷And there was one called Barabbas, who was put in prison with some seditious men, who in the sedition had committed murder. ⁸And when the multitude was come up, they began to desire that he would do as he had ever done unto them. ⁹And Pilate an-

swered them and said: Will you that I release to you the king of the Jews? ¹⁰For he knew that the chief priests had delivered him up out of envy. ¹¹But the chief priests moved the people, that he should rather release Barabbas to them. ¹²And Pilate again answering, saith to them: What will you then that I do to the king of the Jews? ¹³But they again cried out: Crucify him. ¹⁴And Pilate saith to them: Why, what evil hath he done? But they cried out the more: Crucify him.

¹⁵And so Pilate being willing to satisfy the people, released to them Barabbas: and delivered up Jesus, when he had scourged him, to be crucified. ¹⁶And the soldiers led him away into the court of the palace: and they called together the whole band. ¹⁷And they clothe him with purple: and, platting a crown of thorns, they put it upon him. ¹⁸And they began to salute him: Hail, king of the Jews. ¹⁹And they struck his head with a reed: and they did spit on him. And bowing their knees, they adored him.

²⁰And after they had mocked him, they took off the purple from him and put his own garments on him: and they led him out to crucify him. ²¹And they forced one Simon a Cyrenian,

who passed by coming out of the country, the father of Alexander and of Rufus, to take up his cross. ²²And they bring him into the place called Golgotha, which being interpreted is, The place of Calvary.

²³And they gave him to drink wine mingled with myrrh. But he took it not. ²⁴And crucifying him, they divided his garments, casting lots upon them, what every man should take. ²⁵And it was the third hour: and they crucified him.*
²⁶And the inscription of his cause was written over: THE KING OF THE JEWS.

²⁷And with him they crucify two thieves: the one on his right hand, and the other on his left. ²⁸And the scripture was fulfilled, which saith: And with the wicked he was reputed. ²⁹And they that passed by blasphemed him, wagging their heads and saying: Vah, thou that destroyest the temple of God and in three days buildest

---

* *The third hour...* The ancient account divided the day into four parts, which were named from the hour from which they began; the first, third, sixth, and ninth hour. Our Lord was crucified a little before noon; before the third hour had quite expired; but when the sixth hour was near at hand.

it up again: ³⁰Save thyself, coming down from the cross. ³¹In like manner also the chief priests, mocking, said with the scribes one to another: He saved others; himself he cannot save. ³²Let Christ the king of Israel come down now from the cross, that we may see and believe. And they that were crucified with him, reviled him.

³³And when the sixth hour was come, there was darkness over the whole earth until the ninth hour. ³⁴And at the ninth hour, Jesus cried out with a loud voice, saying: Eloi, Eloi, lamma sabacthani? Which is, being interpreted: My God, My God, Why hast thou forsaken me? ³⁵And some of the standers by hearing, said: Behold he calleth Elias. ³⁶And one running and filling a sponge with vinegar and putting it upon a reed, gave him to drink, saying: Stay, let us see if Elias come to take him down. ³⁷And Jesus, having cried out with a loud voice, gave up the ghost.

³⁸And the veil of the temple was rent in two, from the top to the bottom. ³⁹And the centurion who stood over against him, seeing that crying out in this manner he had given up the ghost. said: Indeed this man was the son of

God. ⁴⁰And there were also women looking on afar off: among whom was Mary Magdalen and Mary the mother of James the Less and of Joseph and Salome, ⁴¹Who also when he was in Galilee followed him and ministered to him, and many other women that came up with him to Jerusalem.

⁴²And when evening was now come (because it was the Parasceve, that is, the day before the sabbath), ⁴³Joseph of Arimathea, a noble counsellor, who was also himself looking for the kingdom of God, came and went in boldly to Pilate and begged the body of Jesus. ⁴⁴But Pilate wondered that he should be already dead. And sending for the centurion, he asked him if he were already dead. ⁴⁵And when he had understood it by the centurion, he gave the body to Joseph. ⁴⁶And Joseph, buying fine linen and taking him down, wrapped him up in the fine linen and laid him in a sepulchre which was hewed out of a rock. And he rolled a stone to the door of the sepulchre. ⁴⁷And Mary Magdalen and Mary the mother of Joseph, beheld where he was laid.

THE PASSION OF OUR LORD JESUS CHRIST ACCORDING TO ST LUKE

CHAPTER 22

Now the feast of unleavened bread, which is called the pasch, was at hand. ²And the chief priests and the scribes sought how they might put Jesus to death: but they feared the people.

³And Satan entered into Judas, who was surnamed Iscariot, one of the twelve. ⁴And he went and discoursed with the chief priests and the magistrates, how he might betray him to them. ⁵And they were glad and covenanted to give him money. ⁶And he promised. And he sought opportunity to betray him in the absence of the multitude.

⁷And the day of the unleavened bread came, on which it was necessary that the pasch should

be killed. ⁸And he sent Peter and John, saying: Go, and prepare for us the pasch, that we may eat. ⁹But they said: Where wilt thou that we prepare? ¹⁰And he said to them: Behold, as you go into the city, there shall meet you a man carrying a pitcher of water: follow him into the house where he entereth in. ¹¹And you shall say to the goodman of the house: The master saith to thee: Where is the guest chamber, where I may eat the pasch with my disciples? ¹²And he will shew you a large dining room, furnished. And there prepare. ¹³And they going, found as he had said to them and made ready the pasch.

¹⁴And when the hour was come, he sat down: and the twelve apostles with him. ¹⁵And he said to them: With desire I have desired to eat this pasch with you, before I suffer. ¹⁶For I say to you that from this time I will not eat it, till it be fulfilled in the kingdom of God. ¹⁷And having taken the chalice, he gave thanks and said: Take and divide it among you. ¹⁸For I say to you that I will not drink of the fruit of the vine, till the kingdom of God come.

¹⁹And taking bread, he gave thanks and brake and gave to them, saying: This is my body,

which is given for you. Do this for a commemoration of me.* ²⁰In like manner, the chalice also, after he had supped, saying: This is the chalice, the new testament in my blood, which shall be shed for you.

²¹But yet behold: the hand of him that betrayeth me is with me on the table. ²²And the Son of man indeed goeth, according to that which is determined: but yet, woe to that man by whom he shall be betrayed. ²³And they began to inquire among themselves, which of them it was that should do this thing.

²⁴And there was also a strife amongst them, which of them should seem to be the greater. ²⁵And he said to them: The kings of the Gen-

---

* *Do this for a commemoration of me...* This sacrifice and sacrament is to be continued in the church, to the end of the world, to shew forth the death of Christ, until he cometh. But this commemoration, or remembrance, is by no means inconsistent with the real presence of his body and blood, under these sacramental veils, which represent his death; on the contrary, it is the manner that he himself hath commanded, of commemorating and celebrating his death, by offering in sacrifice, and receiving in the sacrament, that body and blood by which we were redeemed.

tiles lord it over them; and they that have power over them are called beneficent. [26]But you not so: but he that is the greater among you, let him become as the younger: and he that is the leader, as he that serveth. [27]For which is greater, he that sitteth at table or he that serveth? Is not he that sitteth at table? But I am in the midst of you, as he that serveth. [28]And you are they who have continued with me in my temptations: [29]And I dispose to you, as my Father hath disposed to me, a kingdom; [30]That you may eat and drink at my table, in my kingdom: and may sit upon thrones, judging the twelve tribes of Israel.

[31]And the Lord said: Simon, Simon, behold Satan hath desired to have you, that he may sift you as wheat. [32]But I have prayed for thee, that thy faith fail not: and thou, being once converted, confirm thy brethren. [33]Who said to him: Lord, I am ready to go with thee, both into prison and to death. [34]And he said: I say to thee, Peter, the cock shall not crow this day, till thou thrice deniest that thou knowest me. And he said to them:

[35]When I sent you without purse and scrip and shoes, did you want anything? [36]But they said: Nothing. Then said he unto them: But

now he that hath a purse, let him take it, and likewise a scrip: and he that hath not, let him sell his coat and buy a sword. ³⁷For I say to you that this that is written must yet be fulfilled in me. And with the wicked was he reckoned. For the things concerning me have an end. ³⁸But they said: Lord, behold, here are two swords. And he said to them: It is enough.

³⁹And going out, he went, according to his custom, to the Mount of Olives. And his disciples also followed him. ⁴⁰And when he was come to the place, he said to them: Pray, lest ye enter into temptation. ⁴¹And he was withdrawn away from them a stone's cast. And kneeling down, he prayed. ⁴²Saying: Father, if thou wilt, remove this chalice from me: but yet not my will, but thine be done. ⁴³And there appeared to him an angel from heaven, strengthening him. And being in an agony, he prayed the longer.

⁴⁴And his sweat became as drops of blood, trickling down upon the ground. ⁴⁵And when he rose up from prayer and was come to his disciples, he found them sleeping for sorrow. ⁴⁶And he said to them: Why sleep you? Arise: pray: lest you enter into temptation.

⁴⁷As he was yet speaking, behold a multitude; and he that was called Judas, one of the twelve, went before them and drew near to Jesus, for to kiss him. ⁴⁸And Jesus said to him: Judas, dost thou betray the Son of man with a kiss?

⁴⁹And they that were about him, seeing what would follow, said to him: Lord, shall we strike with the sword? ⁵⁰And one of them struck the servant of the high priest and cut off his right ear. ⁵¹But Jesus answering, said: Suffer ye thus far. And when he had touched his ear, he healed him. ⁵²And Jesus said to the chief priests and magistrates of the temple and the ancients, that were come unto him: Are ye come out, as it were against a thief, with swords and clubs? ⁵³When I was daily with you in the temple, you did not stretch forth your hands against me: but this is your hour and the power of darkness.

⁵⁴And apprehending him, they led him to the high priest's house. But Peter followed afar off. ⁵⁵And when they had kindled a fire in the midst of the hall and were sitting about it, Peter was in the midst of them. ⁵⁶Whom when a certain servant maid had seen sitting at the light and had earnestly beheld him, she said: This man

also was with him. ⁵⁷But he denied him, saying: Woman, I know him not. ⁵⁸And after a little while, another seeing him, said: Thou also art one of them. But Peter said: O man, I am not.*
⁵⁹And after the space, as it were of one hour, another certain man affirmed, saying: Of a truth, this man was also with him: for he is also a Galilean. ⁶⁰And Peter said: Man, I know not what thou sayest. And immediately, as he was yet speaking, the cock crew. ⁶¹And the Lord turning looked on Peter. And Peter remembered the word of the Lord, as he had said: Before the

---

* *Another, etc...* Observe here, in order to reconcile the four Evangelists, that divers persons concurred in charging Peter with being Christ's disciple; till at length they brought him to deny him thrice. ¹. The porteress that let him in, and afterwards seeing him at the fire, first put the question to him; and then positively affirmed that he was with Christ. ². Another maid accused him to the standers by; and gave occasion to the man here mentioned to renew the charge against him, which caused the second denial. ³. Others of the company took notice of his being a Galilean; and were seconded by the kinsman of Malchus, who affirmed he had seen him in the garden. And this drew on the third denial.

cock crow, thou shalt deny me thrice. ⁶²And Peter going out, wept bitterly.

⁶³And the men that held him mocked him and struck him. ⁶⁴And they blindfolded him and smote his face. And they asked him saying: Prophesy: Who is it that struck thee? ⁶⁵And blaspheming, many other things they said against him. ⁶⁶And as soon as it was day, the ancients of the people and the chief priests and scribes came together. And they brought him into their council saying: If thou be the Christ, tell us. ⁶⁷And he saith to them: If I shall tell you, you will not believe me. ⁶⁸And if I shall also ask you, you will not answer me, nor let me go. ⁶⁹But hereafter the Son of man shall be sitting on the right hand of the power of God.

⁷⁰Then said they all: Art thou then the Son of God? Who said: You say that I am. ⁷¹And they said: What need we any further testimony? For we ourselves have heard it from his own mouth.

CHAPTER 23

And the whole multitude of them, rising up, led him to Pilate. ²And they began to accuse him, saying: We have found this man perverting our nation and forbidding to give tribute to Caesar and saying that he is Christ the king.

³And Pilate asked him, saying: Art thou the king of the Jews? But he answering, said: Thou sayest it. ⁴And Pilate said to the chief priests and to the multitudes: I find no cause in this man.

⁵But they were more earnest, saying: He stirreth up the people, teaching throughout all Judea, beginning from Galilee to this place. ⁶But Pilate hearing Galilee, asked if the man were of Galilee? ⁷And when he understood that he was of Herod's jurisdiction, he sent him away to Herod, who was also himself at Jerusalem in those days.

⁸And Herod seeing Jesus, was very glad: for he was desirous of a long time to see him, because he had heard many things of him; and he hoped to see some sign wrought by him. ⁹And he questioned him in many words. But he answered him nothing. ¹⁰And the chief priests and the scribes stood by, earnestly accusing him. ¹¹And Herod with his army set him at nought and mocked him, putting on him a white garment: and sent him back to Pilate. ¹²And Herod and Pilate were made friends, that same day: for before they were enemies one to another.

[13]And Pilate, calling together the chief priests and the magistrates and the people, [14]Said to them: You have presented unto me this man as one that perverteth the people. And behold I, having examined him before you, find no cause in this man, in those things wherein you accuse him. [15]No, nor Herod neither. For, I sent you to him: and behold, nothing worthy of death is done to him. [16]I will chastise him therefore and release him.

[17]Now of necessity he was to release unto them one upon the feast day. [18]But the whole multitude together cried out, saying: Away with this man, and release unto us Barabbas: [19]Who, for a certain sedition made in the city and for a murder, was cast into prison. [20]And Pilate again spoke to them, desiring to release Jesus. [21]But they cried again, saying: Crucify him, Crucify him. [22]And he said to them the third time: Why, what evil hath this man done? I find no cause of death in him. I will chastise him therefore and let him go.

[23]But they were instant with loud voices, requiring that he might be crucified. And their voices prevailed. [24]And Pilate gave sentence

that it should be as they required. ²⁵And he released unto them him who for murder and sedition had been cast into prison, whom they had desired. But Jesus he delivered up to their will.

²⁶And as they led him away, they laid hold of one Simon of Cyrene, coming from the country; and they laid the cross on him to carry after Jesus. ²⁷And there followed him a great multitude of people and of women, who bewailed and lamented him. ²⁸But Jesus turning to them, said: Daughters of Jerusalem, weep not over me; but weep for yourselves and for your children. ²⁹For behold, the days shall come, wherein they will say: Blessed are the barren and the wombs that have not borne and the paps that have not given suck. ³⁰Then shall they begin to say to the mountains: Fall upon us. And to the hills: Cover us. ³¹For if in the green wood they do these things, what shall be done in the dry? ³²And there were also two other malefactors led with him to be put to death.

³³And when they were come to the place which is called Calvary, they crucified him there: and the robbers, one on the right hand, and the other on the left. ³⁴And Jesus said: Fa-

ther, forgive them, for they know not what they do. But they, dividing his garments, cast lots.

³⁵And the people stood beholding. And the rulers with them derided him, saying: He saved others: let him save himself, if he be Christ, the elect of God. ³⁶And the soldiers also mocked him, coming to him and offering him vinegar, ³⁷And saying: If thou be the king of the Jews, save thyself.

³⁸And there was also a superscription written over him in letters of Greek and Latin and Hebrew THIS IS THE KING OF THE JEWS.

³⁹And one of those robbers who were hanged blasphemed him, saying: If thou be Christ, save thyself and us. ⁴⁰But the other answering, rebuked him, saying: Neither dost thou fear God, seeing; thou art under the same condemnation? ⁴¹And we indeed justly: for we receive the due reward of our deeds. But this man hath done no evil. ⁴²And he said to Jesus: Lord, remember me when thou shalt come into thy kingdom. ⁴³And Jesus said to him: Amen I say to thee: This day thou shalt be with me in paradise.*

* *In paradise...* That is, in the happy state of rest, joy, and peace everlasting. Christ was pleased,

⁴⁴And it was almost the sixth hour: and there was darkness over all the earth until the ninth hour. ⁴⁵And the sun was darkened, and the veil of the temple was rent in the midst. ⁴⁶And Jesus crying with a loud voice, said: Father, into thy hands I commend my spirit. And saying this, he gave up the ghost.

⁴⁷Now, the centurion, seeing what was done, glorified God, saying: Indeed this was a just man. ⁴⁸And all the multitude of them that were come together to that sight and saw the things that were done returned, striking their breasts. ⁴⁹And all his acquaintance and the women that had followed him from Galilee stood afar off, beholding these things.

⁵⁰And behold there was a man named Joseph who was a counsellor, a good and a just man, ⁵¹(The same had not consented to their counsel

---

by a special privilege, to reward the faith and confession of the penitent thief, with a full discharge of all his sins, both as to the guilt and punishment; and to introduce him immediately after death into the happy society of the saints, whose limbo, that is, the place of their confinement, was now made a paradise by our Lord's going thither.

and doings) of Arimathea, a city of Judea: who also himself looked for the kingdom of God. ⁵²This man went to Pilate and begged the body of Jesus. ⁵³And taking him down, he wrapped him in fine linen and laid him in a sepulchre that was hewed in stone, wherein never yet any man had been laid. ⁵⁴And it was the day of the Parasceve: and the sabbath drew on.* ⁵⁵And the women that were come with him from Galilee, following after, saw the sepulchre and how his body was laid. ⁵⁶And returning, they prepared spices and ointments: and on the sabbath day they rested, according to the commandment.

* *Parasceve...* That is, the eve, or day of preparation for the sabbath.

THE PASSION OF OUR LORD JESUS CHRIST ACCORDING TO ST JOHN

CHAPTER 18

When Jesus had said these things, he went forth with his disciples over the brook Cedron, where there was a garden, into which he entered with his disciples. ²And Judas also, who betrayed him, knew the place: because Jesus had often resorted thither together with his disciples. ³Judas therefore having received a band of soldiers and servants from the chief priests and the Pharisees, cometh thither with lanterns and torches and weapons.

⁴Jesus therefore, knowing all things that should come upon him, went forth and said to them: Whom seek ye? ⁵They answered him: Jesus of Nazareth. Jesus saith to them: I am

he. And Judas also, who betrayed him, stood with them. ⁶As soon therefore as he had said to them: I am he; they went backward and fell to the ground. ⁷Again therefore he asked them: Whom seek ye? And they said: Jesus of Nazareth. ⁸Jesus answered: I have told you that I am he. If therefore you seek me, let these go their way, ⁹That the word might be fulfilled which he said: Of them whom thou hast given me, I have not lost any one.

¹⁰Then Simon Peter, having a sword, drew it and struck the servant of the high priest and cut off his right ear. And the name of the servant was Malchus. ¹¹. Jesus therefore said to Peter: Put up thy sword into the scabbard. The chalice which my father hath given me, shall I not drink it?

¹²Then the band and the tribune and the servants of the Jews took Jesus and bound him. ¹³And they led him away to Annas first, for he was father-in-law to Caiphas, who was the high priest of that year. ¹⁴Now Caiphas was he who had given the counsel to the Jews: That it was expedient that one man should die for the people.

¹⁵And Simon Peter followed Jesus: and so did another disciple. And that disciple was known

to the high priest and went in with Jesus into the court of the high priest. ¹⁶But Peter stood at the door without. The other disciple therefore, who was known to the high priest, went out and spoke to the portress and brought in Peter.

¹⁷The maid therefore that was portress saith to Peter: Art not thou also one of this man's disciples? He saith: I am not. ¹⁸Now the servants and ministers stood at a fire of coals, because it was cold, and warmed themselves. And with them was Peter also, standing and warming himself.

¹⁹The high priest therefore asked Jesus of his disciples and of his doctrine. ²⁰Jesus answered him: I have spoken openly to the world. I have always taught in the synagogue and in the temple, whither all the Jews resort: and in secret I have spoken nothing. ²¹. Why askest thou me? Ask them who have heard what I have spoken unto them. Behold they know what things I have said.

²²And when he had said these things, one of the servants standing by gave Jesus a blow, saying: Answerest thou the high priest so? ²³Jesus answered him: If I have spoken evil, give testimony of the evil; but if well, why strikest thou me?

²⁴And Annas sent him bound to Caiphas the high priest.

²⁵And Simon Peter was standing and warming himself. They said therefore to him: Art not thou also one of his disciples? He denied it and said: I am not. ²⁶One of the servants of the high priest (a kinsman to him whose ear Peter cut off) saith to him: Did not I see thee in the garden with him? ²⁷Again therefore Peter denied: and immediately the cock crew.

²⁸Then they led Jesus from Caiphas to the governor's hall. And it was morning: and they went not into the hall, that they might not be defiled, but that they might eat the pasch.

²⁹Pilate therefore went out to them, and said: What accusation bring you against this man? ³⁰They answered and said to him: If he were not a malefactor, we would not have delivered him up to thee. ³¹Pilate therefore said to them: Take him you, and judge him according to your law. The Jews therefore said to him: It is not lawful for us to put any man to death. ³²That the word of Jesus might be fulfilled, which he said, signifying what death he should die.

³³Pilate therefore went into the hall again and called Jesus and said to him: Art thou the king of the Jews? ³⁴Jesus answered: Sayest thou this thing of thyself, or have others told it thee of me? ³⁵Pilate answered: Am I a Jew? Thy own nation and the chief priests have delivered thee up to me. What hast thou done? ³⁶Jesus answered: My kingdom is not of this world. If my kingdom were of this world, my servants would certainly strive that I should not be delivered to the Jews: but now my kingdom is not from hence. ³⁷Pilate therefore said to him: Art thou a king then? Jesus answered: Thou sayest that I am a king. For this was I born, and for this came I into the world; that I should give testimony to the truth. Every one that is of the truth heareth my voice. ³⁸Pilate saith to him: What is truth?

And when he said this, he went out again to the Jews and saith to them: I find no cause in him. ³⁹But you have a custom that I should release one unto you at the Pasch. Will you, therefore, that I release unto you the king of the Jews? ⁴⁰Then cried they all again, saying: Not this man, but Barabbas. Now Barabbas was a robber.

CHAPTER 19

Then therefore Pilate took Jesus and scourged him. ²And the soldiers platting a crown of thorns, put it upon his head: and they put on him a purple garment. ³And they came to him and said: Hail, king of the Jews. And they gave him blows.

⁴Pilate therefore went forth again and saith to them: Behold, I bring him forth unto you, that you may know that I find no cause in him. ⁵(Jesus therefore came forth, bearing the crown of thorns and the purple garment.) And he saith to them: Behold the Man. ⁶When the chief priests, therefore, and the servants had seen him, they cried out, saying: Crucify him, Crucify him. Pilate saith to them: Take him you, and crucify him: for I find no cause in him. ⁷The Jews answered him: We have a law; and according to the law he ought to die, because he made himself the Son of God.

⁸When Pilate therefore had heard this saying, he feared the more. ⁹And he entered into the hall again; and he said to Jesus: Whence art thou? But Jesus gave him no answer. ¹⁰Pilate therefore saith to him: Speakest thou not

ST JOHN 55

to me? Knowest thou not that I have power to crucify thee, and I have power to release thee? ¹¹. Jesus answered: Thou shouldst not have any power against me, unless it were given thee from above. Therefore, he that hath delivered me to thee hath the greater sin.

¹²And from henceforth Pilate sought to release him. But the Jews cried out, saying: If thou release this man, thou art not Caesar's friend. For whosoever maketh himself a king speaketh against Caesar.

¹³Now when Pilate had heard these words, he brought Jesus forth and sat down in the judgment seat, in the place that is called Lithostrotos, and in Hebrew Gabbatha. ¹⁴And it was the parasceve of the pasch, about the sixth hour: and he saith to the Jews: Behold your king.* ¹⁵But they cried out: Away with him: Away with him: Crucify him. Pilate saith to them: shall I crucify your king? The chief priests answered:

---

* *The parasceve of the pasch...* That is, the day before the paschal sabbath. The eve of every sabbath was called the parasceve, or day of preparation. But this was the eve of a high sabbath, viz., that which fell in the paschal week.

We have no king but Caesar. ¹⁶Then therefore he delivered him to them to be crucified. And they took Jesus and led him forth.

¹⁷And bearing his own cross, he went forth to the place which is called Calvary, but in Hebrew Golgotha. ¹⁸Where they crucified him, and with him two others, one on each side, and Jesus in the midst.

¹⁹And Pilate wrote a title also: and he put it upon the cross. And the writing was: JESUS OF NAZARETH, THE KING OF THE JEWS. ²⁰This title therefore many of the Jews did read: because the place where Jesus was crucified was nigh to the city. And it was written in Hebrew, in Greek, and in Latin. ²¹. Then the chief priests of the Jews said to Pilate: Write not: The King of the Jews. But that he said: I am the King of the Jews. ²²Pilate answered: What I have written, I have written.

²³The soldiers therefore, when they had crucified him, took his garments, (and they made four parts, to every soldier a part) and also his coat. Now the coat was without seam, woven from the top throughout. ²⁴They said then one to another: Let us not cut it but let us cast lots for it, whose it shall be; that the scripture might be

fulfilled, saying: They have parted my garments among them, and upon my vesture they have cast lot. And the soldiers indeed did these things.

²⁵Now there stood by the cross of Jesus, his mother and his mother's sister, Mary of Cleophas, and Mary Magdalen. ²⁶When Jesus therefore had seen his mother and the disciple standing whom he loved, he saith to his mother: Woman, behold thy son. ²⁷After that, he saith to the disciple: Behold thy mother. And from that hour, the disciple took her to his own.

²⁸Afterwards, Jesus knowing that all things were now accomplished, that the scripture might be fulfilled, said: I thirst. ²⁹Now there was a vessel set there, full of vinegar. And they, putting a sponge full of vinegar about hyssop, put it to his mouth. ³⁰Jesus therefore, when he had taken the vinegar, said: It is consummated. And bowing his head, he gave up the ghost.

³¹Then the Jews (because it was the parasceve), that the bodies might not remain upon the cross on the sabbath day (for that was a great sabbath day), besought Pilate that their legs might be broken: and that they might be taken away. ³²The soldiers therefore came: and

they broke the legs of the first, and of the other that was crucified with him. ³³But after they were come to Jesus, when they saw that he was already dead, they did not break his legs. ³⁴But one of the soldiers with a spear opened his side: and immediately there came out blood and water. ³⁵And he that saw it hath given testimony: and his testimony is true. And he knoweth that he saith true: that you also may believe. ³⁶For these things were done that the scripture might be fulfilled: You shall not break a bone of him. ³⁷And again another scripture saith: They shall look on him whom they pierced.

³⁸And after these things, Joseph of Arimathea (because he was a disciple of Jesus, but secretly for fear of the Jews), besought Pilate that he might take away the body of Jesus. And Pilate gave leave. He came therefore and took away the body of Jesus. ³⁹And Nicodemus also came (he who at the first came to Jesus by night), bringing a mixture of myrrh and aloes, about an hundred pound weight. ⁴⁰They took therefore the body of Jesus and bound it in linen cloths, with the spices, as the manner of the Jews is to bury. ⁴¹Now there was in the place where he

was crucified a garden: and in the garden a new sepulchre, wherein no man yet had been laid. ⁴²There, therefore, because of the parasceve of the Jews, they laid Jesus: because the sepulchre was nigh at hand.

www.ingramcontent.com/pod-product-compliance
Lightning Source LLC
Chambersburg PA
CBHW022022290426
44109CB00015B/1275